PERSONAL

FINANCE

For Teens

Introduction

Hey there, fellow teen! Welcome to "Personal Finance for Teens" – your ultimate companion on the thrilling journey to mastering money management and unlocking the door to financial independence.

Have you ever wondered how to make your money work for you? Or perhaps you're eager to learn how to save up for that dream vacation, your college education, or even your first car? Well, you're in the right place! In this book, we'll embark on an exciting adventure together, exploring every aspect of personal finance in a way that's easy to understand, engaging, and tailored just for you.

Throughout these pages, you'll discover practical tips, real-life stories, and actionable advice that will empower you to take control of your finances, set meaningful goals, and chart a course toward a brighter future. Whether you're a seasoned saver or just starting on your financial journey, there's something here for everyone.

But this book is more than just a guide – it's a roadmap to financial freedom. It's about giving you the knowledge, skills, and confidence to make smart decisions with your money, both now and in the years to come. It's about empowering you to live life on your terms, without being held back by financial constraints.

So, get ready to dive in, ask questions, and explore the world of personal finance like never before. Together, we'll learn how to budget like a boss, save like a pro, invest like a guru, and achieve our wildest dreams along the way.

Are you excited? I know I am! So let's buckle up, open our minds, and get ready for the adventure of a lifetime. The journey to financial freedom starts here – are you ready to join me? Let's dive in and make our money work for us!

Broke to Blessed: My Journey with Money

The Wake-Up Call: How I Realized I Needed a Money Makeover

Let me take you back to a moment that changed my financial life forever. It was like any other day, scrolling through social media, dreaming of all the cool stuff I wanted to buy. Then it hit me like a ton of bricks – I was broke. Not just "I can't afford the latest sneakers" broke, but "I can't even buy lunch" broke. It was my wake-up call.

I realized I needed a serious money makeover. It wasn't easy to admit. Who wants to acknowledge they're not in control of their finances? But facing the truth was the first step towards change.

I took a long, hard look at my spending habits. From the daily Starbucks runs to the impulse buys at the mall, I was leaking money faster than a sinking ship. It was time to plug those holes and steer my financial ship back on course.

But it wasn't just about cutting back on expenses. I needed to shift my mindset. Instead of seeing money as something to be wasted, I started to view it as a tool for building the life I wanted. That meant setting goals and making conscious choices about where my money went.

Budgeting became my new best friend. I crafted a simple plan to track my income and expenses, making sure every dollar had a purpose. It wasn't always easy sticking to the budget, but each small victory brought me closer to my goals.

And you know what? Along the way, I discovered something amazing – the power of gratitude. I started appreciating the things I already had instead of constantly chasing more. It was like a weight had been lifted off my shoulders, and I felt lighter, happier, and more in control.

So, fellow teen, if you're feeling stuck in a financial rut, take it from me – your wake-up call could be just around the corner. Embrace it, learn from it, and use it as fuel to ignite your money makeover. You've got this!

Money Mindset Makeover: Shifting from Scarcity to Abundance

Let's talk about something super important: our mindset when it comes to money. Now, I used to think about money in terms of scarcity – like there was never enough to go around. But guess what? I learned that shifting to an abundance mindset can change the game.

Think about it this way: scarcity is like looking at a half-empty glass, always focusing on what you don't have. But abundance? That's seeing the glass as half-full, and recognizing all the opportunities and possibilities around you.

When you have a scarcity mindset, it's easy to feel stressed and worried about money all the time. But when you embrace abundance, you start to see that there's enough for everyone – including you! It's like flipping a switch in your brain from "I can't" to "I can."

So, how do you make the shift? It's all about changing the way you think and talk about money. Instead of saying things like "I'll never be able to afford that," try saying "I'm working towards being able to afford that." See the difference?

Another big part of the money mindset makeover is gratitude. When you're grateful for what you have, you attract more good things into your life. It's like magic! So, take a moment each day to appreciate the money you do have, whether it's a few bucks in your wallet or a roof over your head.

And remember, your worth isn't measured by the amount of money you have. You are valuable and capable of achieving great things, no matter what your bank account says. So, let's shift that mindset from scarcity to abundance and watch as our financial future becomes brighter than ever before!

Budgeting Basics: Creating a Plan for Financial Success

Let's dive into a super important skill that will set you up for financial success: budgeting. Now, I know what you might be thinking – budgeting sounds boring, right? But trust me, it's the key to taking control of your money and reaching your goals.

So, what exactly is budgeting? Think of it like making a plan for your money. Just like you plan out your day or your weekend, a budget helps you decide how you're going to use your money wisely.

First things first, you'll want to know how much money you have coming in each month. This could be from your part-time job, allowance, or any other source of income. Once you've got that figured out, it's time to look at your expenses.

Expenses are all the things you spend money on – like food, clothes, entertainment, and maybe even savings or giving to charity. It's important to track all of your expenses so you know where your money is going.

Now comes the fun part – creating your budget! Start by listing out all of your expenses and how much you typically spend on each one. Then, compare that to your income. Ideally, you want to make sure your expenses don't exceed your income.

If you find that you're spending more than you're making, don't panic! This is where budgeting comes in handy. You can start to look for areas where you can cut back or find ways to increase your income.

But budgeting isn't just about cutting back – it's also about setting priorities. Maybe you're saving up for a new phone or planning a fun trip with friends. By budgeting for these goals, you can make sure you're putting your money towards the things that matter most to you.

And here's the best part – once you've got your budget set up, you can relax knowing that you're in control of your money. No more stressing about where your next dollar is going to come from or feeling guilty about overspending. Budgeting gives you the freedom to live your life on your terms while still working towards your financial goals.

So, fellow teen, are you ready to take the first step towards financial success? Let's get budgeting and watch as our money starts working for us!

Small Wins, Big Impact: Celebrating Financial Milestones

Today, I want to talk to you about something super exciting – celebrating your financial milestones. Now, I know what you might be thinking – milestones are just for big achievements, right? Wrong! Even the smallest wins on your financial journey deserve to be celebrated.

So, what exactly are financial milestones? Well, they're like little checkpoints along the way to reaching your big goals. Whether it's saving your first $100, paying off a credit card, or sticking to your budget for a whole month, each milestone is a step in the right direction.

Why is it important to celebrate these wins? Because it's a reminder that you're making progress! Sometimes, saving money or sticking to a budget can feel like a slog, but celebrating your milestones helps keep you motivated and excited about your financial journey.

Plus, celebrating your wins gives you a chance to reflect on how far you've come. Maybe a few months ago, the idea of saving money seemed impossible, but now you're crushing it! That's something to be proud of.

And here's the best part – celebrating your financial milestones doesn't have to cost a lot of money. It could be as simple as treating yourself to a movie night with friends or having a dance party in your room. The key is to do something that makes you feel good and reminds you of your progress.

So, the next time you hit a financial milestone – big or small – take a moment to pat yourself on the back. You've earned it! And remember, every step you take towards your financial goals brings you one step closer to the life you want to live. Keep up the awesome work, and keep celebrating those wins! You're doing amazing, my friend.

Gratitude and Giving: Finding Joy in Sharing My Wealth

Let's chat about something that's not just about money but about something much bigger – gratitude and giving. Now, you might think that when it comes to money, it's all about what you can get for yourself, right? Well, let me tell you, there's so much joy and fulfillment in sharing your wealth with others.

First off, let's talk about gratitude. It's about being thankful for what you have, no matter how big or small. When you take a moment to appreciate the things you already have – whether it's a loving family, a cozy home, or even just a warm meal – you start to see that you're richer than you might think.

And that's where giving comes in. When you have more than you need, whether it's money, time, or talent, sharing it with others is one of the best feelings in the world. It's like spreading sunshine on a gloomy day – it brightens not just someone else's day, but yours too.

Now, I'm not saying you have to give away all your money or empty out your piggy bank. Giving can be as simple as lending a helping hand to a friend in need, donating clothes you no longer wear or volunteering your time at a local charity.

And here's the cool part – giving doesn't just benefit the person receiving, it benefits you too! Studies have shown that giving can boost your mood, reduce stress, and even improve your physical health. It's like a double dose of feel-good vibes!

So, next time you find yourself with a little extra to spare, think about how you can spread some joy to others. Whether it's donating to a cause you care about or simply showing kindness to someone in need, you'll be amazed at how much happiness it brings – both to them and to you.

Remember, it's not about how much you give, but the intention behind it. So, let's spread a little love, a little kindness, and a little wealth wherever we go. Together, we can make the world a brighter, happier place for everyone.

The Money Puzzle: How I Learned to Budget

Cracking the Code: Understanding Where Your Money Goes

Let's dive into a topic that might seem a bit mysterious at first – understanding where your money goes. You see, just like solving a puzzle, figuring out where your money is going is all about cracking the code.

So, picture this: You're at the mall with your friends, and before you know it, you've spent way more than you planned. Sound familiar? Trust me, I've been there too. But here's the thing – if you want to take control of your money, you've got to know where it's going.

Think of your money as a detective story. Each dollar has its own story to tell – whether it's for food, clothes, entertainment, or savings. And it's up to you to uncover the clues and piece together the puzzle of your spending habits.

One way to crack the code is by tracking your expenses. This could be as simple as jotting down everything you spend money on in a notebook or using a budgeting app on your phone. The key is to be honest with yourself and record every single purchase, no matter how small.

Once you've got a clear picture of where your money is going, it's time to analyze your spending patterns. Are you spending more on clothes than you thought? Are those daily coffee runs adding up? By identifying your spending habits, you can start to make smarter choices about where to put your money.

But here's the thing — cracking the code isn't about beating yourself up over your spending habits. It's about empowering yourself to make better choices in the future. Maybe you realize you're spending too much on takeout, so you start cooking more meals at home. Or perhaps you cut back on impulse buys and start saving for something you want.

The important thing is to keep digging, keep learning, and keep making progress. Just like solving a puzzle, understanding where your money goes takes time and practice. But with a little effort, you'll be a money detective in no time, cracking the code and taking control of your financial future. You've got this!

Setting Priorities: Identifying Needs vs. Wants

Now, I know it can be tempting to spend your cash on all the latest gadgets, fashion trends, and cool stuff you see your friends buying. But here's the thing – not everything you want is something you need.

So, how do you tell the difference between needs and wants? It's all about asking yourself a few simple questions. A need is something essential for your survival or well-being – like food, shelter, clothing, and healthcare. These are things you can't live without.

On the other hand, a want is something you desire or wish for, but it's not necessary for your basic needs. Think of it as the "extras" in life – like the latest smartphone, designer clothes, or tickets to a concert. While wants can bring joy and excitement, they're not essential for your day-to-day life.

Now, don't get me wrong – it's okay to indulge in wants now and then. But when it comes to managing your money wisely, it's important to prioritize your needs first. That means making sure you have enough money to cover essentials like food, housing, and healthcare before splurging on wants.

Setting priorities also means thinking about your long-term goals and how your spending choices align with them. Maybe you're saving up for college, a car, or your place someday. By prioritizing your needs over your wants, you can free up more money to put towards your goals and dreams.

But here's the cool part – once you've taken care of your needs and set aside money for your goals, you can still enjoy your wants guilt-free! It's all about finding the right balance between taking care of your responsibilities and treating yourself to the things that bring you joy.

So, the next time you're tempted to splurge on something shiny and new, take a moment to think about whether it's a need or a want. By setting priorities and making smart choices with your money, you'll be well on your way to financial success. You've got this!

Making It Work: Finding Creative Ways to Stick to Your Budget

I know, I know, the word "budget" might sound like a buzzkill, but trust me, it's the secret sauce to managing your money like a boss.

Now, sticking to your budget doesn't mean you have to give up all the fun stuff in life. It's all about finding creative ways to make it work – kind of like solving a puzzle or coming up with a cool DIY project.

One way to make it work is by getting creative with your spending. Instead of blowing all your cash on expensive outings with friends, why not suggest budget-friendly alternatives? Think picnics in the park, movie nights at home, or DIY spa days. You'll save money while still having a blast with your buddies.

Another trick is to look for ways to cut costs without sacrificing quality. Maybe you can find cheaper alternatives to your favorite brands, shop during sales, or take advantage of discounts and coupons. With a little creativity, you can stretch your dollars further without feeling like you're missing out.

And here's a fun idea – turn sticking to your budget into a game! Challenge yourself to see how much you can save each week or month, and reward yourself with a little treat when you hit your goals. It's like turning budgeting into a fun challenge with awesome prizes at the end.

But perhaps the most important thing when it comes to sticking to your budget is staying motivated. Remember why you set your budget in the first place – whether it's to save up for something special, achieve a financial goal, or just feel more in control of your money. Keeping your eye on the prize will help you stay focused and committed, even when temptation strikes.

So, fellow teen, are you ready to get creative and make your budget work for you? With a little imagination and determination, you'll be a budgeting pro in no time. And who knows? You might even discover some new hobbies, make amazing memories, and unlock a whole new world of possibilities along the way. You've got this!

Adjusting and Adapting: Fine-Tuning Your Budget Over Time

You see, setting a budget is just the first step on your financial journey. As you go along, life might throw you a few curveballs, and that's okay! The key is to be flexible and willing to fine-tune your budget over time.

Think of your budget as a roadmap for your money. It's there to guide you towards your goals and help you stay on track. But just like a real roadmap, sometimes you might need to take a detour or change your route to reach your destination.

Maybe you get a raise at your part-time job, or maybe you have some unexpected expenses pop up – like a car repair or a school trip. When life changes, your budget might need to change too. And that's where adjusting and adapting comes in.

The first step is to take a look at your budget and see where you might need to make changes. Are there areas where you can cut back to make room for new expenses? Or maybe you need to reassess your priorities and shift your spending accordingly.

But here's the cool part – adjusting your budget doesn't have to mean giving up the things you love. It's all about finding a balance that works for you. Maybe you can find ways to save money in one area so you can still afford to splurge on your favorite hobbies or treats.

And remember, your budget isn't set in stone. It's a living, breathing document that can change and evolve with you. So don't be afraid to experiment, try new things, and see what works best for your unique situation.

The most important thing is to stay proactive and keep an eye on your finances regularly. By staying flexible and willing to adapt, you'll be better prepared to handle whatever life throws your way – whether it's a financial setback or a new opportunity. So, fellow teen, are you ready to fine-tune your budget and keep crushing your financial goals? Let's do this!

Budgeting Tools and Apps: Harnessing Technology for Financial Management

Now, I know the idea of managing your money might sound a bit daunting but fear not! With the help of technology, budgeting has never been easier – or more fun!

Imagine having your personal finance assistant right at your fingertips, ready to help you track your spending, set savings goals, and stay on budget. Well, with budgeting tools and apps, that's exactly what you get!

One of the best things about budgeting apps is how easy they are to use. Gone are the days of manually tracking your expenses or scribbling numbers on a piece of paper. With just a few taps on your phone, you can see exactly where your money is going and how it's stacking up against your budget.

But that's not all – budgeting apps also come with a bunch of handy features to help you stay on track. From customizable spending categories to automatic transaction syncing, these apps make it a breeze to manage your money like a pro.

Plus, many budgeting apps offer helpful insights and analysis to help you make smarter financial decisions. Want to know how much you're spending on groceries each month? Or how do your spending habits compare to others your age? With just a few clicks, you can find out!

But perhaps the best part of all is the motivation and accountability that budgeting apps provide. With colorful charts, progress trackers, and friendly reminders, these apps keep you motivated to stick to your budget and reach your financial goals.

So, whether you're saving up for a big purchase, planning for college, or just trying to get a handle on your spending, budgeting tools, and apps are your secret weapon for financial success. So why not give one a try? You'll be amazed at how much easier – and even fun – managing your money can be with a little help from technology. Ready to take control of your finances like a boss? Let's do this!

Piggy Banks and Beyond: My Savings Adventure

Building Blocks: Starting Your Savings Journey

Now, I know saving money might not sound like the most exciting thing in the world, but trust me, it's the secret sauce to achieving your dreams and living life on your terms.

Think of saving money like planting seeds in a garden. Each dollar you save is like planting a tiny seed that has the potential to grow into something amazing. Whether it's saving up for a new phone, a car, or even your place someday, every dollar you set aside brings you one step closer to your goals.

But where do you start? Well, it's all about taking that first step – no matter how small. Maybe you start by setting aside a portion of your allowance or paycheck each week. Even if it's just a few bucks, it adds up over time!

Another way to kickstart your savings journey is by setting specific goals. What are you saving for? Maybe it's a short-term goal like buying concert tickets or a new video game, or maybe it's a long-term goal like saving for college or traveling the world. By having clear goals in mind, you'll stay motivated and focused on your savings journey.

And here's a fun idea – why not make saving money a game? Challenge yourself to see how much you can save each month, and reward yourself when you hit your goals. It's like turning saving money into a fun challenge with awesome prizes at the end!

But perhaps the most important thing when it comes to saving money is consistency. Make saving a habit by setting aside a little bit of money each time you get paid, and watch as your savings grow over time. Remember, Rome wasn't built in a day – and neither is a healthy savings account!

So, fellow teen, are you ready to start your savings journey? Whether you're saving up for something big or just looking to build your financial security, taking that first step is the key to unlocking a world of possibilities. So why wait? Let's start saving and watch as our dreams become reality!

The Power of Consistency: Making Saving a Habit

I know saving money might seem like a big task, but trust me, it's all about making it a habit – just like brushing your teeth or checking your phone in the morning.

Consistency is like the secret ingredient that makes saving money work. It's about committing yourself to set aside a little bit of money regularly, whether it's weekly, biweekly, or monthly. And here's the cool part – the more consistent you are, the easier it becomes!

So, how do you make saving money a habit? It's all about finding a routine that works for you. Maybe you decide to set aside a portion of your allowance or paycheck every time you get paid. Or perhaps you automate your savings by setting up a direct deposit from your checking account to your savings account. Whatever method you choose, the key is to stick with it – no matter what.

But here's the thing – consistency doesn't mean you have to save huge amounts of money every time. Even setting aside a small amount regularly can add up over time. It's like building a snowball – the more you roll it, the bigger it gets!

And here's another tip – make saving money fun! Challenge yourself to see how much you can save each month, and reward yourself when you hit your goals. Maybe you treat yourself to a movie night with friends or buy yourself something special. By turning saving money into a game, you'll stay motivated and excited about your progress.

But perhaps the most important thing when it comes to consistency is perseverance. There might be times when it feels tough to stick to your savings plan – maybe you have unexpected expenses or temptation strikes. But don't give up! Remember why you started saving in the first place and keep pushing forward. Consistency is the key to unlocking your financial goals and building a brighter future for yourself. So, fellow teen, are you ready to make saving money a habit? Let's do this!

Emergency Funds: Why Every Teen Needs One

Now it might sound a bit boring, but trust me, having an emergency fund is like having a superhero cape for your finances – it's there to save the day when you least expect it.

So, what exactly is an emergency fund? It's a stash of money set aside for unexpected expenses or emergencies – like if your phone suddenly stops working, your laptop crashes or your car needs repairs. Having an emergency fund means you won't have to stress about how to pay for these unexpected costs – you've got it covered!

But why does every teen need an emergency fund? Well, think about it this way – life is full of surprises, and not all of them are good. Maybe your parents can't help out in a pinch, or you don't want to rely on them for every little expense. Having your emergency fund gives you peace of mind knowing that you can handle whatever life throws your way – all on your own.

And here's the cool part – starting an emergency fund is easier than you might think. You don't need to be rolling in dough to get started – even setting aside a small amount regularly can add up over time. Whether it's a portion of your

allowance, money from your part-time job, or spare change
you find lying around, every little bit counts!

But perhaps the best thing about having an emergency fund
is the sense of security and independence it brings. Knowing
that you have money set aside for emergencies means you
can focus on enjoying life and pursuing your dreams without
worrying about what might happen if something goes wrong.

So, fellow teen, are you ready to take control of your finances
and build your emergency fund? It's like having a safety net to
catch you if you fall – and trust me, it's a game-changer. So
start small, stay consistent, and watch as your emergency fund
grows – you'll thank yourself later!

Saving for Dreams: Setting Goals and Making Them a Reality

Whether it's traveling the world, buying your dream car, or going to college, we all have dreams and aspirations that we want to turn into reality. And guess what? Saving money is the key to making those dreams come true!

So, where do you start? Well, it's all about setting goals. Think about what you want to achieve – maybe it's a short-term goal like saving up for a new phone or a concert ticket, or maybe it's a long-term goal like buying a car or going to college. Whatever it is, having clear goals in mind will help you stay focused and motivated on your savings journey.

Once you've set your goals, it's time to make a plan. How much money do you need to save to reach your goal? And how long will it take you to get there? Break down your goal into smaller, manageable steps, and set deadlines for each one. This will help you stay on track and measure your progress along the way.

But here's the fun part – saving for your dreams doesn't have to be boring! Get creative with your savings plan and find ways to make it fun. Challenge yourself to see how much you can save each week or month, and reward yourself when you hit your goals. Maybe you treat yourself to a movie night with friends or buy yourself something special. By turning saving money into a game, you'll stay motivated and excited about your progress.

And remember, saving for your dreams is all about priorities. Maybe you have to make some sacrifices along the way – like cutting back on eating out or skipping that expensive coffee shop. But trust me, it'll all be worth it when you reach your goal and turn your dreams into reality.

So, fellow teen, are you ready to start saving for your dreams? With a little planning, determination, and creativity, you can achieve anything you set your mind to. So why wait? Let's start saving and watch as our dreams become reality!

Supercharging Your Savings: Tips and Tricks to Grow Your Money Faster

Let's kick things up a notch and talk about supercharging your savings. Saving money can sometimes feel like watching paint dry – slow and boring. But fear not! With a few tips and tricks up your sleeve, you can grow your money faster than you ever thought possible.

First off, let's talk about interest. You see when you put your money into a savings account, it doesn't just sit there collecting dust – it earns interest! Interest is like free money that the bank pays you for keeping your money with them. And the best part? The longer you leave your money in the bank, the more interest it earns. It's like watching your savings grow on autopilot!

But here's the thing – not all savings accounts are created equal. Some banks offer higher interest rates than others, so it's worth shopping around to find the best deal. Look for accounts that offer competitive interest rates and low fees, so you can maximize your earnings without sacrificing accessibility.

Another way to supercharge your savings is by automating your deposits. Set up a recurring transfer from your checking account to your savings account each time you get paid. That way, you'll never forget to save – it'll happen automatically, like magic!

And here's a fun idea – why not try your hand at investing? Investing is like planting seeds in a garden – except instead of growing plants, you're growing your money! Whether it's stocks, bonds, or mutual funds, investing gives your money the potential to grow faster than it would in a savings account. Just remember, investing comes with risks, so make sure you do your research and only invest money you can afford to lose.

But perhaps the most important thing when it comes to supercharging your savings is consistency. Keep making regular deposits into your savings account, even when it feels like you're not making much progress. Remember, every dollar counts, and over time, those small contributions will add up to big results.

So, fellow teen, are you ready to supercharge your savings and watch your money grow faster than ever? With a little know-how and a lot of determination, you can achieve your financial goals in no time. So why wait? Let's start supercharging and watch as our savings soar to new heights!

From Rookie to Investor: My First Steps in the Stock Market

Investing 101: Understanding the Basics of Investing

The word "investing" might sound a bit intimidating at first, but trust me, it's not as complicated as it seems. Understanding the basics of investing can set you up for a brighter financial future.

So, what exactly is investing? Think of it like planting seeds in a garden – except instead of growing plants, you're growing your money! When you invest, you're putting your money into something with the hope that it will grow over time and provide you with a return on your investment.

There are lots of different things you can invest in, like stocks, bonds, mutual funds, and real estate. Each type of investment comes with its level of risk and potential return, so it's important to do your research and choose investments that align with your goals and risk tolerance.

One of the most common types of investments for beginners is stocks. When you buy a stock, you're essentially buying a small piece of ownership in a company. If the company does well, the value of your stock goes up – and vice versa. Stocks can be a great way to grow your money over the long term, but they also come with a higher level of risk.

Another popular investment option is bonds. When you buy a bond, you're essentially loaning money to a government or corporation in exchange for regular interest payments. Bonds are generally considered safer than stocks because they offer a fixed rate of return, but they also tend to have lower potential returns.

Mutual funds are another great option for beginner investors. A mutual fund is a pool of money from many investors that is invested in a diversified portfolio of stocks, bonds, or other assets. This helps spread out the risk and can provide more stable returns over time.

But perhaps the most important thing to remember when it comes to investing is to start small and stay diversified. Don't put all your eggs in one basket – spread out your investments across different asset classes and industries to reduce risk. And remember, investing is a long-term game – don't get discouraged by short-term fluctuations in the market. With patience, discipline, and a little bit of know-how, you can build a solid investment portfolio that will help you achieve your financial goals. So why wait? Let's start investing and watch as our money grows!

Exploring Investment Options: Stocks, Bonds, and Mutual Funds

Each of these options offers a unique way to grow your money and achieve your financial goals, so let's dive in and explore what they're all about.

First up, let's talk about stocks. When you buy a stock, you're essentially buying a small piece of ownership in a company. That means you get to share in the company's success – if the company does well, the value of your stock goes up, and you could potentially earn dividends, which are a share of the company's profits. Stocks can be a great way to grow your money over the long term, but they also come with a higher level of risk, as the value of your investment can fluctuate with the market.

Next, let's talk about bonds. When you buy a bond, you're essentially loaning money to a government or corporation in exchange for regular interest payments. Bonds are generally considered safer than stocks because they offer a fixed rate of return and are less volatile. They can be a great option for investors looking for more stability in their portfolio, but they tend to offer lower potential returns compared to stocks.

Finally, let's talk about mutual funds. A mutual fund is a pool of money from many investors that is invested in a diversified portfolio of stocks, bonds, or other assets. This helps spread out the risk and can provide more stable returns over time. Mutual funds are a great option for beginner investors because they offer instant diversification and are managed by professional fund managers who make investment decisions on behalf of the investors.

So, which investment option is right for you? Well, that depends on your financial goals, risk tolerance, and investment timeline. If you're looking for high growth potential and are willing to take on more risk, stocks might be the way to go. If you're looking for more stability and steady income, bonds might be a better fit. And if you want instant diversification and professional management, mutual funds could be the answer.

The important thing is to do your research, understand your options, and choose investments that align with your goals and risk tolerance. And remember, investing is a long-term game – don't get discouraged by short-term fluctuations in the market. With patience, discipline, and a little bit of know-how, you can build a solid investment portfolio that will help you achieve your financial dreams. So why wait? Let's start exploring our investment options and watch as our money grows!

Risk vs. Reward: Finding Your Comfort Zone

So, what exactly do I mean by risk vs. reward? Well, it's all about weighing the potential risks and rewards of different financial choices. You see, every decision you make with your money comes with some level of risk – whether it's saving, investing, or spending. And the potential rewards vary depending on how much risk you're willing to take.

Let's break it down a bit. Saving money in a bank account is generally considered low-risk. Sure, you might not earn as much interest as you would with other investments, but your money is safe and secure. On the other hand, investing in the stock market or starting a business comes with higher risk – there's a chance you could lose money. But the potential rewards can be much greater if things go well.

So, how do you find your comfort zone when it comes to risk vs. reward? It's all about knowing yourself and your financial goals. Are you someone who likes to play it safe and prefers steady, predictable returns? Or are you more of a risk-taker who's willing to take chances for the chance of higher rewards?

There's no right or wrong answer – it's all about finding what works best for you. Maybe you start by dipping your toes into the world of investing with a small amount of money, or maybe you prefer to stick with safer options until you feel more comfortable. The key is to know your limits and not take on more risk than you can afford to lose.

But here's the thing – taking some risks can be a good thing. It's how you grow and learn and, sometimes, achieve your biggest dreams. Just make sure you're making informed decisions and not gambling with money you can't afford to lose.

So, fellow teen, are you ready to find your comfort zone when it comes to risk vs. reward? Whether you're playing it safe or taking a chance on something new, remember to stay true to yourself and your financial goals. With a little courage and a lot of smarts, you'll be well on your way to financial success. Let's do this!

Getting Started: Opening Your First Investment Account

The idea of investing might sound a bit intimidating at first, but trust me, it's not as complicated as it seems. It's a great way to grow your money and set yourself up for a bright financial future.

So, what exactly is an investment account? Well, it's like a special savings account where you can put your money into different investments – like stocks, bonds, or mutual funds. Instead of just sitting in a regular savings account, your money has the potential to grow faster over time through the power of investing.

But where do you start? The first step is to choose the right type of investment account for you. There are lots of options out there, from individual brokerage accounts to retirement accounts like IRAs and 401(k)s. Each type of account has its benefits and restrictions, so it's important to do your research and find the one that's best suited to your needs and goals.

Once you've chosen the right type of investment account, it's time to open it up! This usually involves filling out some paperwork and providing some personal information, like your name, address, and social security number. It's a bit like opening a bank account, but for investing instead.

Next, you'll need to fund your investment account. This is where you transfer money from your regular bank account into your new investment account. You can start with as little or as much as you like – it's totally up to you!

Now comes the fun part – choosing your investments. You'll have lots of options to choose from, including stocks, bonds, mutual funds, and more. Each type of investment comes with its level of risk and potential return, so it's important to do your research and choose wisely.

But remember, investing isn't about getting rich quickly – it's about growing your money over time through smart, informed decisions. So take your time, do your homework, and don't be afraid to ask for help if you need it. With a little patience and perseverance, you'll be well on your way to building wealth and achieving your financial goals. So, fellow teen, are you ready to open your first investment account and start building your financial future? Let's do this!

Learning from Mistakes: Embracing the Ups and Downs of Investing

Making mistakes might not sound like the most fun thing in the world, but trust me, it's all part of the journey to becoming a savvy investor.

You see, investing isn't always smooth sailing. Just like anything else in life, you're bound to hit a few bumps along the way. Maybe you pick a stock that doesn't perform as well as you hoped, or maybe you panic and sell your investments when the market dips. It happens to the best of us!

But here's the thing – making mistakes is a good thing. It's how we learn and grow and become better investors. Instead of beating yourself up over your mistakes, embrace them as valuable learning experiences.

So, what can you learn from your investing mistakes? Well, for starters, you can learn to be more patient and disciplined. Investing is a long-term game, and trying to time the market or chase hot stocks rarely pays off in the end. By staying calm and sticking to your investment strategy, you'll be better equipped to weather the ups and downs of the market.

You can also learn to do your homework and research before making investment decisions. Instead of blindly following the latest investment fads or tips from friends, take the time to thoroughly research your investments and understand what you're getting into. Knowledge is power when it comes to investing, and the more you know, the better equipped you'll be to make smart decisions with your money.

But perhaps the most important thing you can learn from your investing mistakes is resilience. No matter how experienced or knowledgeable you are, you're bound to encounter setbacks and failures along the way. But instead of letting them discourage you, use them as fuel to keep pushing forward and striving for success.

So, fellow teen, are you ready to embrace the ups and downs of investing and turn your mistakes into valuable lessons? Remember, every mistake is just another step on the path to becoming a confident and successful investor. So keep learning, keep growing, and never be afraid to take a chance on yourself and your financial future. You've got this!

Debt Detour: Navigating the Ups and Downs

Debt Awareness: Recognizing Different Types of Debt

So, what exactly is debt? Debt is money that you owe to someone else – like a bank, a credit card company, or even a friend or family member. It's like borrowing money with the promise to pay it back later, usually with interest.

Now, there are different types of debt, and it's important to recognize the differences between them. One common type of debt is called "good debt." This is debt that's used to finance something that has the potential to increase in value over time – like a college education or a home. Good debt can be a smart investment in your future, as long as you can afford to repay it and it helps you achieve your goals.

On the other hand, there's also "bad debt." This is debt that's used to finance things that decrease in value over time – like clothes, gadgets, or vacations. Bad debt usually comes with high-interest rates and can quickly spiral out of control if you're not careful. It's like digging yourself into a hole that's hard to climb out of.

Another type of debt is called "secured debt." This is debt that's backed by collateral – like a house or a car. If you fail to repay the debt, the lender can take possession of the collateral as repayment. Secured debt usually comes with lower interest rates because it's less risky for the lender.

Finally, there's "unsecured debt." This is debt that's not backed by collateral – like credit card debt or personal loans. Because there's no collateral to back it up, unsecured debt usually comes with higher interest rates and stricter repayment terms.

So, why is it important to be aware of different types of debt? Well, understanding the differences can help you make smarter financial decisions and avoid getting into debt you can't afford to repay. By using debt responsibly and only borrowing what you need and can afford to repay, you'll set yourself up for a brighter financial future. So, fellow teen, are you ready to become debt-savvy and take control of your finances? Let's do this!

The Debt Trap: Understanding the Consequences of Borrowing

You see, borrowing money might seem like a quick fix when you're in a pinch, but it can lead to a whole lot of trouble if you're not careful.

First off, let's talk about what borrowing means. When you borrow money, you're taking out a loan – whether it's from a bank, a credit card company, or even a friend or family member. And while it might seem like free money at the time, it's important to remember that you'll have to pay it back – often with interest!

Now, there are lots of different types of borrowing, from credit cards and personal loans to student loans and mortgages. Each type of debt comes with its terms and conditions, so it's important to read the fine print and understand what you're getting into before you borrow.

But here's the thing – borrowing money isn't always a bad thing. Sometimes, it's necessary – like taking out student loans to pay for college or getting a mortgage to buy a home. The key is to borrow responsibly and only take on debt that you can afford to repay.

So, what are the consequences of borrowing? Well, for starters, borrowing money means you'll have to pay it back – plus interest. That means you'll end up paying more for whatever you bought in the long run. If you can't afford to make your payments on time, you could end up damaging your credit score, which can make it harder to borrow money in the future.

But perhaps the biggest consequence of borrowing is the stress and anxiety that comes with carrying debt. Constantly worrying about how you're going to make your payments or how you're going to dig yourself out of debt can take a toll on your mental and emotional well-being.

So, fellow teen, before you borrow money, take a moment to think about the consequences. Is it worth it? Can you afford to repay it? Are there other options available to you? By borrowing responsibly and understanding the consequences, you'll be better equipped to make smart financial decisions and build a brighter future for yourself.

Creating a Repayment Plan: Strategies for Tackling Debt

I know debt might seem overwhelming, but trust me, you've got the power to take control of it and turn things around.

First things first, take a deep breath. It's important to face your debt head-on, but it's equally important not to let it stress you out too much. You're not alone in this, and there are strategies you can use to make things easier.

The first step is to gather all the information about your debts. Make a list of who you owe money to, how much you owe, and the interest rates on each debt. This will give you a clear picture of where you stand and help you prioritize which debts to tackle first.

Once you have all the details, it's time to come up with a plan of attack. There are a few different strategies you can use, but one popular approach is called the debt snowball method. With this method, you focus on paying off your smallest debt first while making minimum payments on your other debts. Once the smallest debt is paid off, you roll that payment into paying off the next smallest debt, and so on. It's like building momentum as you go, and it can be super motivating to see your debts disappearing one by one.

Another approach is called the debt avalanche method. With this method, you focus on paying off your debt with the highest interest rate first while making minimum payments on your other debts. Once the highest-interest debt is paid off, you move on to the next highest-interest debt, and so on. This method can save you money on interest in the long run, but it might not feel as rewarding in the short term since it takes longer to see progress on your debts.

Whichever method you choose, the key is to stick with it and stay disciplined. Cut back on unnecessary expenses, look for ways to increase your income, and put any extra money towards your debts. And don't forget to celebrate your progress along the way – even small victories deserve to be celebrated!

Remember, getting out of debt won't happen overnight, but with patience, perseverance, and a solid repayment plan, you'll get there sooner than you think. You've got this!

Avoiding Debt Traps: Smart Ways to Manage Your Finances

It can be tempting to spend money on all the latest gadgets, fashion trends, and cool stuff you see your friends buying. But trust me, falling into debt traps can cause a whole lot of stress and trouble down the road.

So, how do you avoid these debt traps and keep your finances in check? It's all about being smart with your money and making wise decisions.

First things first, it's important to live within your means. That means not spending more money than you have. It can be tempting to whip out your credit card for that shiny new thing you've been eyeing, but if you can't afford to pay for it in full when the bill comes, it's probably best to hold off.

Next, it's important to budget your money wisely. Take the time to track your income and expenses, and make a plan for how you'll spend and save your money each month. Budgeting might sound boring, but trust me, it's the key to staying on top of your finances and avoiding debt traps.

Another smart move is to build an emergency fund. Having a stash of money set aside for unexpected expenses can be a lifesaver when things don't go as planned. Aim to save up enough to cover three to six months' worth of living expenses – that way, you'll be prepared for whatever life throws your way.

And finally, it's important to be mindful of your spending habits. Take a look at where your money is going each month and identify any areas where you might be overspending. Maybe you can cut back on eating out, cancel subscriptions you don't use, or find cheaper alternatives to your favorite brands. Small changes can add up to big savings over time!

Remember, managing your finances wisely isn't about depriving yourself of the things you love – it's about making smart choices that will set you up for a bright financial future. So, take control of your money, avoid those debt traps, and watch as your financial goals become a reality. You've got this!

Building Credit: Using Debt Responsibly to Build a Positive Credit History

The idea of using debt responsibly might sound a bit scary, but trust me, it's a key step in establishing a positive credit history and unlocking financial opportunities down the road.

First things first, let's talk about what credit is. Credit is your ability to borrow money or access goods and services with the understanding that you'll pay for them later. It's like a financial reputation – lenders use your credit history to determine whether they'll lend you money and what interest rate they'll charge you.

So, why is having good credit important? Well, it can open doors for you in the future. Whether you want to buy a car, rent an apartment, or get a cell phone plan, having good credit can make things a whole lot easier. Plus, it can save you money in the long run by qualifying you for lower interest rates and better loan terms.

But how do you build credit as a teenager? One common way is by getting a credit card. Now, I know what you're thinking – isn't that just asking for trouble? But here's the thing – when used responsibly, a credit card can be a powerful tool for building credit.

Start by applying for a student credit card or a secured credit card with a low credit limit. Use it to make small purchases that you can afford to pay off in full each month. This shows lenders that you're responsible with your credit and can help you establish a positive credit history.

Another way to build credit is by taking out a small loan – like a student loan or a car loan – and making regular, on-time payments. This demonstrates to lenders that you're able to manage different types of debt responsibly, which can boost your credit score over time.

But here's the most important thing to remember – building credit takes time and patience. It's not something that happens overnight, so don't get discouraged if you don't see results right away. Just keep making smart financial decisions, and before you know it, you'll have built a solid credit history that opens doors to a world of opportunities. So, are you ready to start building credit and taking control of your financial future? Let's do this!

Taxes and Tangles: My Tax Time Tales

Decoding Taxes: Understanding the Basics of Taxation

Taxes might seem like a confusing and boring topic, but trust me, understanding the basics of taxation is a crucial life skill that'll come in handy as you grow older.

So, what exactly are taxes? Well, taxes are fees that we pay to the government to fund public services and programs. These services include things like schools, roads, hospitals, and public safety. Taxes help keep our communities running smoothly and ensure that everyone has access to the resources they need.

But how do taxes work? There are different types of taxes, but the most common ones are income taxes, sales taxes, and property taxes.

Income taxes are taxes that you pay on the money you earn from working. When you get a paycheck from your job, your employer withholds a portion of your earnings to pay for federal and state income taxes. The amount of tax you owe depends on how much you earn and other factors like deductions and credits.

Sales taxes, on the other hand, are taxes that you pay when you buy goods and services. These taxes are added to the price of the items you purchase and are collected by the seller. Sales tax rates vary depending on where you live and what you're buying.

And finally, there are property taxes, which are taxes that you pay on the value of your home or other real estate property. These taxes help fund local services like schools, libraries, and parks and are usually based on the assessed value of your property.

Now, I know taxes might seem like a hassle, but they're a vital part of our society. By paying taxes, we all contribute to the greater good and help build stronger, more vibrant communities for everyone.

But here's the good news – there are ways to make taxes less daunting. Take the time to educate yourself about how taxes work and what you can do to minimize your tax burden. And don't be afraid to ask for help if you need it – whether it's from a trusted adult, a tax professional, or good old Google.

So, fellow teen, are you ready to decode the mysteries of taxes and become a savvy taxpayer? With a little knowledge and a willingness to learn, you'll be well on your way to mastering the art of taxation. Let's do this!

Tax Forms and Filing: Navigating the Maze of Tax Documents

Let's tackle another important aspect of taxes – tax forms and filing. The idea of dealing with tax documents might seem overwhelming, but don't worry, I've got your back. I'm here to help you navigate the maze of tax forms and make the filing process as smooth as possible.

First things first, let's talk about the most common tax form you'll encounter – the Form 1040. This is the main form used by individuals to file their federal income taxes. It asks for information about your income, deductions, credits, and other relevant financial details.

Now, depending on your financial situation, you might also need to fill out additional forms and schedules. For example, if you have income from investments or self-employment, you might need to fill out Schedule D or Schedule C, respectively. If you have dependents, you'll need to fill out additional forms to claim tax benefits like the Child Tax Credit or the Earned Income Tax Credit.

But don't worry if this all sounds a bit overwhelming – there are plenty of resources available to help you navigate the process. The IRS website, for example, has tons of helpful information and resources to guide you through the filing process. You can also consider using tax preparation software or hiring a tax professional to help you with your taxes.

When it comes time to file your taxes, you have a few options. You can file electronically using tax preparation software or the IRS's free file program. This is generally the fastest and most convenient option, and it also helps reduce the risk of errors on your tax return.

Alternatively, you can file a paper tax return by mail. This option takes a bit longer, but it's still a valid way to file your taxes if you prefer the old-school approach.

Whichever method you choose, make sure to double-check all your information before submitting your tax return. Mistakes can delay your refund or even trigger an audit, so it's important to take your time and review everything carefully.

And remember, filing your taxes doesn't have to be a dreaded chore – it's just another part of adulting. So take a deep breath, gather your documents, and tackle those tax forms like a boss. You've got this!

Tax Deductions and Credits: Maximizing Your Tax Benefits

Now, I know taxes can be a bit of a drag, but these little gems can help you save money and maximize your tax benefits. So, let's dive in and learn how to make the most of them!

First off, let's talk about tax deductions. A tax deduction is an expense that you can subtract from your taxable income, reducing the amount of income that's subject to taxes. It's like getting a discount on your taxes for certain expenses you incur throughout the year.

Common tax deductions include things like charitable contributions, mortgage interest, medical expenses, and certain education expenses. So, if you donated money to charity, paid interest on your student loans, or had a big medical bill, you might be able to deduct those expenses from your taxable income and lower your tax bill.

But wait, it gets even better – let's talk about tax credits. Unlike deductions, which reduce the amount of income that's subject to taxes, tax credits are a dollar-for-dollar reduction in the amount of taxes you owe. In other words, they're like free money from the government!

There are lots of different tax credits out there, but some common ones for teens include the Child Tax Credit, the Earned Income Tax Credit, and the American Opportunity Tax Credit for college expenses. These credits can help offset the cost of raising a family, working, or paying for higher education.

So, how do you make sure you're taking full advantage of these tax benefits? Well, it's important to keep good records of your expenses throughout the year and to familiarize yourself with the tax deductions and credits you might be eligible for. That way, when it comes time to file your taxes, you can claim all the deductions and credits you're entitled to and maximize your tax benefits.

And here's a pro tip – consider using tax preparation software or hiring a tax professional to help you navigate the world of tax deductions and credits. They can help ensure you're taking advantage of all the tax benefits available to you and help you maximize your refund.

So, fellow teen, are you ready to start maximizing your tax benefits and putting more money back in your pocket? With a little knowledge and a bit of planning, you can make tax time a little less painful and keep more of your hard-earned money where it belongs – in your wallet! Let's do this!

Tax Planning: Strategies for Minimizing Your Tax Burden

So, what is tax planning? Well, it's the process of organizing your finances in a way that helps you legally minimize your tax liability. In other words, it's about finding ways to pay less in taxes while still staying on the right side of the law.

One common tax planning strategy is to take advantage of tax-advantaged accounts. These are special types of accounts that offer tax benefits like tax-deferred growth or tax-free withdrawals. Examples include retirement accounts like IRAs and 401(k)s, health savings accounts (HSAs), and education savings accounts like 529 plans. By contributing to these accounts, you can reduce your taxable income and save money on taxes both now and in the future.

Another tax planning strategy is to time your income and deductions strategically. For example, if you expect to be in a higher tax bracket next year, you might consider deferring some income until the following year or accelerating some deductions into the current year to lower your taxable income. This can help you take advantage of lower tax rates and maximize your tax savings.

It's also important to stay informed about changes to the tax laws and how they might affect you. Tax laws are constantly changing, and what worked for you last year might not work for you this year. So, take the time to educate yourself about any changes to the tax code and how they might impact your tax situation.

And finally, don't forget to consult with a tax professional if you need help with your tax planning. They can provide personalized advice based on your unique financial situation and help you make smart decisions that minimize your tax burden and maximize your tax savings.

So, fellow teen, are you ready to start tax planning like a pro and keep more of your hard-earned money in your pocket? With a little knowledge and a bit of planning, you can minimize your tax burden and set yourself up for financial success. Let's do this!

Tax Responsibilities: Learning to Fulfill Your Civic Duty

Understanding your tax responsibilities is a key part of being a responsible citizen and contributing to society.

So, what exactly are tax responsibilities? Well, as a citizen, you must pay taxes on your income and any other taxable earnings you may have. This money goes towards funding important public services and programs that benefit everyone, like schools, roads, healthcare, and public safety.

But it's not just about paying taxes – it's also about fulfilling your civic duty and being honest and transparent in your tax dealings. That means accurately reporting your income, deductions, and credits on your tax return and paying the correct amount of taxes owed.

Now, I know taxes can be a bit confusing, especially when you're just starting. But don't worry – there are lots of resources available to help you navigate the tax system and fulfill your responsibilities.

For starters, familiarize yourself with the basics of taxation and how taxes work. The IRS website has tons of helpful information and resources, including guides, tutorials, and interactive tools to help you understand your tax obligations.

It's also a good idea to keep organized records of your income and expenses throughout the year. That way, when it comes time to file your taxes, you'll have all the information you need to accurately report your income and claim any deductions or credits you're entitled to.

And don't forget to file your taxes on time! The deadline for filing your federal income tax return is usually April 15th, although it can vary depending on the year and your circumstances. Failing to file your taxes on time can result in penalties and interest charges, so make sure to mark your calendar and get your taxes done ahead of time.

Finally, if you have any questions or concerns about your taxes, don't hesitate to reach out for help. Whether it's from a trusted adult, a tax professional, or the IRS itself, there are plenty of resources available to answer your questions and ensure you're fulfilling your tax responsibilities.

So, fellow teen, are you ready to fulfill your civic duty and take responsibility for your taxes? With a little knowledge and a willingness to learn, you'll be well on your way to becoming a responsible taxpayer and contributing member of society. Let's do this!

Goal Getter: Chasing Dreams with Dollars

Dream Big, Start Small: Setting SMART Financial Goals

Whether you dream of traveling the world, buying your dream car, or going to college, setting SMART financial goals can help you get there.

So, what exactly are SMART goals? SMART stands for Specific, Measurable, Achievable, Relevant, and Time-bound. Let's break it down:

Specific: Your goals should be clear and specific. Instead of saying, "I want to save money," try saying, "I want to save $500 for a new phone."

Measurable: Your goals should be quantifiable so you can track your progress. Break your goal down into smaller milestones and set deadlines for each one.

Achievable: Your goals should be realistic and attainable. While it's great to dream big, setting goals that are too lofty can set you up for disappointment. Start small and work your way up.

Relevant: Your goals should align with your values and priorities. Think about what's important to you and focus on goals that will help you achieve those things.

Time-bound: Your goals should have a deadline. Setting a timeframe for achieving your goals will help keep you motivated and focused.

Now that you know what SMART goals are, it's time to start setting them. Take some time to think about what you want to achieve financially – maybe it's saving for a car, paying for college, or starting your own business. Once you've identified your goals, break them down into smaller, more manageable tasks and set deadlines for each one.

For example, if your goal is to save $1,000 for a summer trip, break it down into smaller milestones, like saving $100 per month for the next 10 months. Then, set reminders for yourself to track your progress and adjust your plan as needed.

Remember, Rome wasn't built in a day, and neither are financial goals. It's okay to start small and work your way up – the important thing is to get started and stay committed. And don't forget to celebrate your progress along the way – every milestone you reach is a step closer to achieving your dreams.

So, fellow teen, are you ready to dream big and start small? With SMART financial goals, you can turn your dreams into reality and create the future you've always imagined. Let's do this!

Visualizing Success: Creating a Vision Board for Your Financial Goals

So, what exactly is a vision board? A vision board is a visual representation of your goals, dreams, and aspirations. It's like a collage of images, words, and phrases that inspire and motivate you to take action toward achieving your goals.

Creating a vision board for your financial goals is a great way to stay focused and keep your dreams front and center in your mind. Plus, it's a fun and creative way to express yourself and tap into your imagination.

Here's how to get started:

First, gather your materials. You'll need a poster board or canvas, magazines or printed images, scissors, glue or tape, and markers or pens.

Next, think about your financial goals and what you want to achieve. Do you want to save money for a car, go on a dream vacation, or start your own business? Whatever your goals are, think about the images, words, and phrases that represent them.

Now, start flipping through magazines or searching online for images and words that resonate with you. Cut out any images or words that speak to your goals and aspirations, and arrange them on your poster board or canvas.

Get creative! Add color, doodles, and embellishments to make your vision board uniquely yours. Don't be afraid to think outside the box and let your imagination run wild.

Once you're happy with your vision board, hang it somewhere you'll see it every day – like your bedroom wall or workspace. Take a few moments each day to look at your vision board and visualize yourself achieving your goals. Imagine how it will feel when you accomplish what you've set out to do, and let that feeling inspire and motivate you to take action.

And remember, your vision board is a work in progress. As you achieve your goals and set new ones, update your vision board to reflect your evolving dreams and aspirations.

So, fellow teen, are you ready to unleash your creativity and visualize success? With a little imagination and a lot of determination, you can use your vision board to turn your financial goals into reality. Let's get crafting!

Breaking It Down: Turning Big Goals into Manageable Steps

I know it can be overwhelming to think about big goals, like saving for college or starting your own business, but trust me, breaking them down into smaller steps can make them much more achievable.

So, what exactly does it mean to break down your goals? Well, it's all about taking a big, daunting goal and breaking it into smaller, more manageable tasks. Think of it like climbing a mountain – if you try to tackle the whole thing at once, it can feel overwhelming. But if you break it down into smaller steps – like hiking to the first lookout point, then the next, and so on – it becomes much more manageable.

Let's say, for example, your goal is to save $1,000 for a new laptop. Instead of focusing on the $1,000 as one big, intimidating number, break it down into smaller, more manageable steps. Start by figuring out how much you can realistically save each month, then set aside that amount of money from your income or allowance. Maybe you can cut back on eating out or entertainment expenses to free up some extra cash for savings.

Next, set up a separate savings account specifically for your laptop fund. This will help you keep track of your progress and resist the temptation to dip into your savings for other things.

Once you've got your savings plan in place, set smaller milestones along the way to keep yourself motivated. Maybe your first milestone is saving $100, then $250, then $500, and so on. Celebrate each milestone you reach – whether it's treating yourself to a small reward or simply patting yourself on the back for a job well done.

Breaking down your goals into manageable steps not only makes them more achievable but also helps you stay focused and motivated along the way. Instead of feeling overwhelmed by the enormity of your goals, you can take things one step at a time and build momentum as you go.

So, fellow teen, are you ready to break down your big goals into manageable steps? With a little planning, determination, and perseverance, you can achieve anything you set your mind to. Let's break it down and get started on the path to success!

Tracking Progress: Keeping Yourself Accountable Along the Way

It can be easy to get caught up in the day-to-day hustle and forget about the bigger picture, but keeping track of your progress is key to staying on track and reaching your goals.

So, why is tracking progress important? Well, for starters, it helps you stay accountable to yourself. When you track your progress, you can see how far you've come and how much closer you are to achieving your goals. It's like having a roadmap that guides you along your journey and keeps you focused on the destination.

Tracking progress also helps you identify what's working and what's not. If you're making steady progress towards your goals, great – keep doing what you're doing! But if you're falling behind or encountering obstacles along the way, tracking your progress can help you pinpoint where things went wrong and make adjustments as needed.

So, how do you track your progress? There are lots of different ways to do it, so choose a method that works best for you. Some people like to use a journal or planner to write down their goals and track their progress over time. Others prefer to use apps or online tools to keep track of their goals and set reminders for themselves.

Whatever method you choose, make sure to set regular check-ins with yourself to review your progress and make any necessary adjustments to your plan. Maybe you set aside time each week to reflect on your progress and update your goals accordingly. Or maybe you check in with yourself every month to assess how things are going and set new goals for the coming weeks.

And don't forget to celebrate your progress along the way! Whether it's reaching a milestone, hitting a new personal best, or simply sticking to your plan for another day, take the time to acknowledge your achievements and give yourself a pat on the back. You've worked hard to get where you are, and you deserve to celebrate your success.

So, fellow teen, are you ready to start tracking your progress and holding yourself accountable along the way? With a little consistency and determination, you can stay on track and achieve anything you set your mind to. Let's track our progress and crush those goals!

Celebrating Achievements: Rewarding Yourself for Reaching Milestones

I know it can be easy to get caught up in the hustle of chasing your goals, but it's important to take the time to acknowledge and celebrate your successes along the way.

So, why is it important to celebrate your achievements? Well, for starters, celebrating your successes helps boost your confidence and motivation. When you take the time to acknowledge your achievements, no matter how big or small, it reminds you of your capabilities and encourages you to keep pushing forward toward your goals.

Celebrating your achievements also helps you stay focused and motivated. It gives you something to look forward to and helps break up the monotony of working towards your goals. Plus, it's a great way to reward yourself for all your hard work and dedication.

So, how do you celebrate your achievements? Well, that's totally up to you! It could be something simple, like treating yourself to your favorite dessert or taking a day off to relax and recharge. Or it could be something more extravagant, like planning a weekend getaway or splurging on that thing you've been wanting for ages.

The important thing is to find ways to celebrate that resonate with you and make you feel good about your accomplishments. Maybe you like to celebrate with friends and family, or maybe you prefer to celebrate solo – whatever works for you is okay!

And don't forget to celebrate all your achievements, no matter how big or small. Whether you've reached a major milestone or just made progress toward your goals, take the time to acknowledge your hard work and give yourself a pat on the back. You deserve it!

So, fellow teen, are you ready to start celebrating your achievements and rewarding yourself for reaching milestones? With a little celebration and self-care, you can stay motivated and inspired on your journey towards success. Let's celebrate our achievements and keep crushing those goals!

Magic Money: The Compound Interest Chronicles

The Power of Compound Interest: Understanding How Your Money Grows

The idea of interest might not sound very exciting, but trust me, understanding how compound interest works can be a game-changer when it comes to building wealth over time.

So, what exactly is compound interest? Well, it's interest on top of interest – in other words, it's interest that's earned not only on the initial amount of money you invest or save but also on any interest that's been added to that amount over time. It's like a snowball effect – the more money you have saved or invested, and the longer it's been growing, the more interest you'll earn.

Let's break it down with an example. Say you invest $100 in a savings account that earns 5% interest per year. At the end of the first year, you'll earn $5 in interest, bringing your total savings to $105. But here's where it gets interesting – in the second year, you'll earn 5% interest not only on your initial $100 but also on the $5 of interest you earned in the first year. So, instead of earning $5 in interest again, you'll earn $5.25, bringing your total savings to $110.25. And the cycle continues – the longer your money stays invested, the more it grows thanks to the power of compound interest.

Now, you might be thinking, "But I'm just a teenager – why should I care about compound interest?" Well, here's the thing – the earlier you start saving and investing, the more time your money has to grow thanks to compound interest. Even small amounts of money invested early on can grow into significant sums over time, thanks to the magic of compounding.

So, how can you take advantage of compound interest as a teenager? Start by saving and investing regularly, even if it's just a small amount each month. Whether you're putting money into a savings account, a retirement account, or the stock market, the key is to start early and stay consistent. The longer your money has to grow, the more powerful compound interest becomes.

And don't forget to reinvest your earnings! Instead of withdrawing the interest you earn, reinvest it back into your savings or investments to maximize the power of compound interest.

So, fellow teen, are you ready to harness the power of compound interest and watch your money grow over time? With a little patience and discipline, you can leverage the magic of compounding to build wealth and secure your financial future. Let's start investing in our future selves and reaping the rewards of compound interest!

Starting Early: Leveraging Time to Maximize Your Returns

Why is starting early so important? Well, it all comes down to the power of time. The earlier you start saving and investing, the more time your money has to grow and compound. And as we just talked about, compound interest is like a snowball rolling downhill – the longer it rolls, the bigger it gets.

Let me give you an example to illustrate this point. Let's say you start investing $100 per month at age 18 and continue investing until you're 28, for a total of 10 years. Then, you stop investing altogether and let your money sit and grow. Meanwhile, your friend decides to wait until they're 28 to start investing and invests $100 per month until they're 65, for a total of 37 years.

Now, who do you think will end up with more money in the end? Surprisingly, it's you! Even though you only invested for 10 years compared to your friend's 37 years, the power of starting early and letting your money compound over time means that you'll end up with more money in the end.

But here's the catch – to take advantage of the power of starting early, you need to start now. The longer you wait to start saving and investing, the less time your money has to grow and compound. And that means you'll have to save and invest more money later on to achieve the same results.

So, what can you do to start early and maximize your returns? Start by setting aside a portion of your income for savings and investing, even if it's just a small amount each month. Whether you're putting money into a savings account, a retirement account, or the stock market, the key is to start now and stay consistent.

And don't be discouraged if you can't save or invest a lot right away – every little bit helps, and the important thing is to get started and let time do the rest.

So, fellow teen, are you ready to start early and leverage time to maximize your returns? With a little patience and discipline, you can set yourself up for a bright financial future and achieve your goals faster than you ever thought possible. Let's start now and watch our money grow over time!

The Rule of 72: A Simple Trick to Estimate Investment Growth

Let me introduce you to a super handy trick called the Rule of 72. It's like a secret weapon that can help you estimate how long it will take for your investments to double in value.

So, here's how it works: the Rule of 72 is a quick and easy way to estimate the number of years it will take for an investment to double, given a fixed annual rate of return. All you have to do is divide 72 by the annual rate of return, and the result will give you the approximate number of years it will take for your investment to double.

For example, let's say you're investing money in the stock market and you expect to earn an average annual return of 8%. To estimate how long it will take for your investment to double, simply divide 72 by 8, which equals 9. So according to the Rule of 72, it will take approximately 9 years for your investment to double in value.

Pretty cool, right? The Rule of 72 is a simple and handy tool that can help you get a rough estimate of how your investments will grow over time. It's not perfect, of course – actual investment returns can vary based on several factors –

but it's a great starting point for planning and setting financial goals.

Now, you might be wondering why it's called the Rule of 72. Well, it's because 72 is a convenient number that's easy to divide by many common interest rates. Plus, it's close enough to the actual doubling time for most practical purposes.

So, the next time you're thinking about investing or planning for your financial future, remember the Rule of 72. It's a simple trick that can help you estimate how long it will take for your investments to double and set realistic expectations for your financial goals.

And who knows? Maybe someday you'll be able to use the Rule of 72 to estimate how long it will take for your investments to grow into a small fortune. With a little patience and the power of compound interest on your side, anything is possible!

So, fellow teen, are you ready to add the Rule of 72 to your financial toolkit and start estimating your investment growth like a pro? With this simple trick, you'll be well on your way to understanding how your money can work for you and achieving your financial goals faster than you ever thought possible. Let's dive in and start estimating those investment returns!

Harnessing Compound Interest: Strategies for Long-Term Wealth Building

Let's dive deeper into the amazing world of compound interest and explore some strategies for harnessing its power to build long-term wealth. Compound interest is like a superhero in the world of finance – it has the power to turn small investments into big returns over time.

One of the best strategies for harnessing compound interest is to start early and invest regularly. As we talked about earlier, the longer your money has to grow and compound, the more powerful it becomes. So, the earlier you start investing, even if it's just a small amount each month, the more time your money will have to work its magic and grow into a substantial sum over time.

Another strategy is to reinvest your earnings. Instead of withdrawing the interest or dividends you earn on your investments, reinvest them back into your portfolio. This allows your earnings to compound over time and accelerate the growth of your investments. It's like adding fuel to the fire – the more you reinvest, the faster your wealth will grow.

Diversification is another key strategy for long-term wealth building. Instead of putting all your eggs in one basket, spread your investments across a variety of assets, such as stocks, bonds, real estate, and mutual funds. This helps reduce the risk of loss and ensures that your portfolio is well-positioned to weather any market fluctuations.

Consistency is also important when it comes to harnessing compound interest. Stick to your investment plan and continue investing regularly, even when the market is volatile or your financial situation changes. Remember, it's the long-term trend that matters most, so stay focused on your goals and keep moving forward.

Lastly, don't forget to review and adjust your investment strategy periodically. As your financial situation changes and your goals evolve, it's important to reassess your investment portfolio and make any necessary adjustments to ensure that it continues to align with your objectives.

So, fellow teen, are you ready to harness the power of compound interest and start building long-term wealth? With a little patience, consistency, and smart investing strategies, you can set yourself up for a bright financial future and achieve your goals faster than you ever thought possible. Let's harness the power of compound interest and start building our wealth today!

Patience Pays Off: Embracing the Journey to Financial Independence

It can be tempting to want instant gratification and see results right away, but the truth is, that building wealth and achieving financial independence takes time and patience.

Think of it like planting a garden. You can't expect to see flowers blooming overnight – it takes time for seeds to sprout, plants to grow, and flowers to blossom. Similarly, building wealth requires patience and persistence. It's about making smart choices, staying disciplined, and trusting the process, even when it feels like progress is slow.

So, why is patience so important when it comes to financial independence? Well, for starters, building wealth is a long-term journey, not a sprint. It's about making consistent, sustainable progress over time, rather than trying to get rich quickly. And that takes patience – the patience to stick to your investment plan, weather market fluctuations, and stay focused on your goals, even when the going gets tough.

Patience also allows you to make better decisions. When you're patient, you're less likely to make impulsive or emotional decisions based on short-term fluctuations in the market. Instead, you can take a step back, evaluate your options, and make decisions that are in line with your long-term goals and objectives.

And perhaps most importantly, patience allows you to enjoy the journey. Building wealth and achieving financial independence is about more than just reaching a destination – it's about the experiences, lessons, and growth that happen along the way. By embracing patience, you can appreciate the progress you've made, celebrate your successes, and stay motivated to keep moving forward, even when the road ahead seems long.

So, fellow teen, are you ready to embrace patience and embark on the journey to financial independence? Remember, Rome wasn't built in a day, and neither is wealth. With a little patience, persistence, and determination, you can achieve anything you set your mind to. Let's embrace the journey and enjoy the ride!

Stormy Seas: Weathering Financial Risks

Identifying Risks: Recognizing Potential Threats to Your Finances

It might not be the most exciting topic, but understanding and recognizing potential threats to your financial security is key to protecting yourself and your future.

So, what exactly are these risks we're talking about? Well, several types of risks could impact your finances, including:

First, there's the risk of unexpected expenses. Life is full of surprises, and sometimes those surprises come with a hefty price tag – like a medical emergency, car repairs, or home maintenance issues. These unexpected expenses can quickly derail your budget and leave you scrambling to cover the costs.

Next, there's the risk of loss in the stock market. Investing in the stock market can be a great way to grow your wealth over time, but it also comes with risks. The value of stocks and other investments can fluctuate based on market conditions, economic factors, and other external forces. And while historically, the stock market has provided solid returns over the long term, there's always the potential for losses, especially in the short term.

Another risk to consider is the risk of inflation. Inflation is the gradual increase in prices over time, which erodes the purchasing power of your money. Inflation can eat away at your savings and investments, making it harder to achieve your financial goals if you're not prepared for it.

And let's not forget about the risk of debt. Taking on too much debt, whether it's credit card debt, student loans, or a mortgage, can put a strain on your finances and make it difficult to achieve financial stability. High levels of debt can lead to financial stress, missed payments, and even bankruptcy if not managed properly.

So, how can you protect yourself against these risks? Well, the first step is to be aware of them and understand how they could impact your finances. Once you've identified the potential threats, you can take steps to mitigate the risks and protect yourself against financial hardship.

For example, you could build an emergency fund to cover unexpected expenses, diversify your investments to spread out the risk, and stay on top of inflation by investing in assets that have historically outpaced inflation over time.

You can also avoid taking on too much debt by living within your means, budgeting carefully, and only borrowing what you can afford to repay. And don't forget to review your insurance coverage regularly to make sure you're adequately protected against unexpected events like illness, accidents, or natural disasters.

By identifying risks and taking proactive steps to protect yourself, you can safeguard your finances and set yourself up for a more secure financial future. So, fellow teen, are you ready to take control of your finances and protect yourself against potential threats? With a little awareness and planning, you can navigate the ups and downs of life with confidence and resilience. Let's identify those risks and take steps to protect ourselves against financial hardship!

Building Resilience: Creating a Financial Safety Net

Creating a financial safety net to help you weather life's unexpected storms.

So, what exactly is a financial safety net? Well, think of it like a cushion or a backup plan that you can rely on when things don't go as planned. It's about having enough savings and resources to cover your basic needs and expenses, even if you hit a rough patch or encounter unexpected challenges.

Building resilience starts with saving money. Set aside a portion of your income each month, even if it's just a small amount, and gradually build up your savings over time. Aim to save enough to cover at least three to six months' worth of living expenses – this will give you a buffer to fall back on in case of emergencies, like losing your job or facing unexpected medical bills.

Next, consider investing in insurance to protect yourself against unexpected events. Health insurance, auto insurance, renters, or homeowners insurance – these are all important forms of protection that can help cover the costs of accidents, illnesses, or property damage. While insurance premiums can seem like an extra expense, they provide valuable peace of mind and financial protection when you need it most.

It's also important to have a plan for managing debt. While some forms of debt, like student loans or a mortgage, can be a necessary part of achieving your goals, too much debt can be a burden that weighs you down. Make a plan to pay off high-interest debt as quickly as possible, and avoid taking on new debt unless necessary.

Finally, don't forget to invest in yourself and your skills. Building resilience isn't just about having money in the bank – it's also about having the knowledge, skills, and resources to adapt and thrive in any situation. Invest in your education, your health, and your personal development, and you'll be better equipped to handle whatever life throws your way.

So, fellow teen, are you ready to build resilience and create a financial safety net for yourself? By saving money, investing in insurance, managing debt, and investing in yourself, you can build a solid foundation for financial stability and weather life's storms with confidence. Let's start building that safety net and protecting our financial future today!

Insurance Essentials: Protecting Yourself Against Life's Uncertainties

So, what exactly is insurance? Well, think of it like a safety net or a shield that helps protect you financially in case of unexpected events, like accidents, illnesses, or property damage. By paying a small amount of money, called a premium, to an insurance company, you can transfer the risk of these events to them and receive financial compensation if something bad happens.

There are several types of insurance that you might need, depending on your circumstances:

First, there's health insurance. Health insurance helps cover the costs of medical care, like doctor's visits, prescription medications, and hospital stays. Having health insurance can help protect you from high medical bills and ensure that you have access to the care you need when you need it.

Next, there's auto insurance. If you own a car or drive regularly, auto insurance is a must-have. Auto insurance helps cover the costs of repairs or replacement if your car is damaged or stolen, as well as medical expenses if you're injured in an accident. It's not just a legal requirement in many places – it's also a smart way to protect yourself and your finances on the road.

If you rent your home, renters insurance is another important form of protection. Renters insurance helps cover the costs of replacing your belongings if they're damaged or stolen, as well as liability protection in case someone is injured in your home. It's an affordable way to protect your possessions and your peace of mind.

And if you own a home, homeowners insurance is essential. Homeowners insurance helps cover the costs of repairing or rebuilding your home if it's damaged or destroyed by fire, natural disasters, or other covered events. It also provides liability protection in case someone is injured on your property.

There are other types of insurance too, like life insurance, disability insurance, and umbrella insurance, which provide additional liability coverage beyond what's covered by your other policies. The key is to assess your needs and choose the right types and amounts of insurance to protect yourself and your finances.

So, fellow teen, are you ready to take control of your financial future and protect yourself against life's uncertainties? By understanding the basics of insurance and choosing the right coverage for your needs, you can build a solid foundation for financial security and peace of mind. Let's make sure we're covered and ready for whatever life throws our way!

Diversification: Spreading Your Investments to Minimize Risk

It might sound fancy, but it's pretty simple and incredibly important for managing risk and maximizing returns.

So, what exactly is diversification? Well, think of it like not putting all your eggs in one basket. Instead of investing all your money in just one type of asset, like stocks or real estate, diversification means spreading your investments across a variety of different assets.

Why is diversification important? Well, it's all about managing risk. You see, different types of investments tend to behave differently in different market conditions. For example, while stocks might perform well during periods of economic growth, bonds might provide stability during times of market volatility. By diversifying your investments across different asset classes, you can reduce the overall risk in your portfolio and increase the likelihood of achieving consistent returns over time.

But diversification isn't just about spreading your investments across different types of assets – it's also about diversifying within asset classes. For example, if you're investing in stocks, you might diversify across different industries, sectors, and geographic regions. This helps further reduce the risk of your portfolio being overly dependent on the performance of just a few individual stocks.

So, how can you diversify your investments as a teenager? Well, one option is to invest in mutual funds or exchange-traded funds (ETFs), which are investment vehicles that pool together money from many investors to invest in a diversified portfolio of assets. By investing in mutual funds or ETFs, you can gain exposure to a wide range of assets without having to pick individual stocks or bonds yourself.

Another option is to consider investing in a target-date fund, which is a type of mutual fund that automatically adjusts its asset allocation over time based on your target retirement date. Target-date funds typically start with a more aggressive asset allocation when you're young and gradually shift towards a more conservative allocation as you approach retirement age.

The key is to assess your risk tolerance, investment goals, and time horizon, and choose a diversified portfolio that aligns with your needs and objectives. By diversifying your investments, you can reduce the risk of your portfolio and increase the likelihood of achieving your financial goals over the long term.

So, fellow teen, are you ready to embrace the power of diversification and build a well-rounded investment portfolio? By spreading your investments across different asset classes and within asset classes, you can minimize risk and maximize returns, setting yourself up for a brighter financial future. Let's diversify our investments and take control of our financial destiny!

Staying Vigilant: Monitoring and Adapting to Changing Financial Landscapes

Staying vigilant, in other words, keeping an eye on things and being proactive about adapting to changes in the financial landscape.

You see, the world of finance is always changing. Interest rates go up and down, stock markets fluctuate, and economic conditions shift. And while you can't predict the future, you can stay vigilant and be prepared to adapt to whatever comes your way.

So, how can you stay vigilant when it comes to your finances? Well, one way is to keep track of your spending and savings. By monitoring your income and expenses regularly, you can identify any areas where you might be overspending or where you could potentially save more money. This can help you stay on track with your financial goals and make adjustments as needed.

It's also important to stay informed about what's happening in the world of finance. Keep up with the news, read financial publications, and stay educated about economic trends and developments. This can help you anticipate changes in the financial landscape and make informed decisions about your investments and financial decisions.

Another way to stay vigilant is to regularly review and update your financial plan. As your circumstances change and your goals evolve, it's important to reassess your financial situation and make any necessary adjustments to your plan. This might involve revisiting your budget, reallocating your investments, or updating your savings goals.

And don't forget to stay vigilant about protecting yourself against fraud and identity theft. Keep your personal information safe, monitor your accounts for any suspicious activity, and report any unauthorized transactions to your bank or credit card company immediately.

By staying vigilant and proactive about monitoring and adapting to changing financial landscapes, you can better protect yourself and your finances against unexpected challenges and seize opportunities for growth and success. So, fellow teen, are you ready to stay vigilant and take control of your financial future? Let's stay informed, stay proactive, and stay vigilant, so we can navigate the ever-changing world of finance with confidence and resilience!

Captain of My Ship: Sailing Towards Financial Freedom

Defining Financial Freedom: What Does it Mean to You?

Well, it's different for everyone, but at its core, financial freedom is about having enough money and resources to live life on your terms, without being held back by financial constraints.

For some people, financial freedom might mean being able to pursue their passions and interests without having to worry about money. It could mean traveling the world, starting their own business, or pursuing higher education without being burdened by student loan debt.

For others, financial freedom might mean having the freedom to make choices that align with their values and priorities. It could mean being able to support their family, give back to their community, or pursue meaningful work that makes a difference in the world.

But no matter what financial freedom looks like to you, one thing is for sure – it's about more than just having a lot of money. It's about having the freedom and flexibility to live the life you want, without being limited by financial constraints.

So, how can you achieve financial freedom as a teenager? Well, it starts with setting goals and making a plan. Think about what financial freedom means to you and what steps you need to take to get there. Maybe it means saving a certain amount of money each month, investing in your education or skills, or starting a side hustle to earn extra income.

It also means being smart about your money and making wise financial decisions. That means living within your means, avoiding debt whenever possible, and making saving and investing a priority. It might not always be easy, but with determination and discipline, you can achieve financial freedom and create the life you've always dreamed of.

So, fellow teen, what does financial freedom mean to you? Take some time to think about your goals and priorities, and start taking steps to make them a reality. With hard work, determination, and a little bit of patience, you can achieve financial freedom and create the life you've always dreamed of. Let's define our version of financial freedom and start working towards it today!

Creating Your Financial Blueprint: Mapping Out Your Journey to Freedom

Think of it like a roadmap that will guide you on your journey to financial freedom. It's all about setting goals, making a plan, and taking action to achieve your dreams.

So, how do you create your financial blueprint? Well, it starts with setting clear and specific goals. What do you want to achieve with your money? Do you want to save for college, buy a car, travel the world, or start your own business? Take some time to think about your short-term and long-term goals and write them down.

Once you have your goals in mind, it's time to make a plan. Start by assessing your current financial situation. How much money do you have coming in each month, and how much do you have going out? Take a look at your income, expenses, savings, and debt, and see where you stand.

Next, think about what steps you need to take to achieve your goals. Do you need to save more money, earn extra income, invest in your education, or pay off debt? Break down your goals into smaller, manageable steps, and create a timeline for achieving them.

It's also important to think about how you'll track your progress along the way. Set up a system for monitoring your income, expenses, savings, and investments, and regularly review your financial plan to make sure you're on track to meet your goals.

And don't forget to be flexible and adapt your plan as needed. Life is full of unexpected twists and turns, and your financial situation may change over time. Be prepared to reassess your goals and adjust your plan accordingly to stay on course.

By creating your financial blueprint, you're taking control of your financial future and setting yourself up for success. It might not always be easy, but with determination, discipline, and a clear plan in place, you can achieve your goals and create the life you've always dreamed of.

So, fellow teen, are you ready to create your financial blueprint and map out your journey to freedom? With clear goals, a solid plan, and the determination to succeed, you can achieve anything you set your mind to. Let's start mapping out our journey to financial freedom today!

Building Multiple Income Streams: Diversifying Your Revenue Streams

You see, having more than one way to make money is like having multiple doors open to opportunities and financial stability. It's all about diversifying your revenue streams to create more security and flexibility in your life.

So, why is it important to build multiple income streams? Well, think about it like this: if one of your income streams dries up or slows down, you'll still have other streams flowing in to support you. It's like having a safety net that can catch you if you fall.

Now, you might be wondering how to build multiple income streams as a teenager. Well, there are plenty of ways to do it! One option is to explore different ways to earn money beyond just a traditional job. You could start a side hustle, like tutoring, pet sitting, or selling handmade crafts online. Or, you could look for freelance gigs or part-time work in your community.

Another option is to invest in assets that generate passive income, like stocks, bonds, or real estate. Passive income is money that you earn without actively working for it, and it can be a great way to build wealth over time. You could also consider starting a small business or investing in a rental property to generate additional streams of income.

The key is to be creative and open-minded about the possibilities. Think about your skills, interests, and resources, and look for opportunities to leverage them to create new income streams. And don't be afraid to start small – even a little extra money coming in each month can add up over time and provide more financial security.

But remember, building multiple income streams takes time and effort. It's not something that happens overnight, and it requires dedication, perseverance, and a willingness to take risks. But the rewards can be well worth it – more financial freedom, greater flexibility, and the ability to pursue your passions and interests on your terms.

So, fellow teen, are you ready to start building multiple income streams and diversifying your revenue streams? With a little creativity, hustle, and determination, you can create more security and flexibility in your life and open up new doors of opportunity. Let's start exploring the possibilities and building our financial future today!

Living Below Your Means: Embracing Frugality for Long-Term Success

Now, I know it might not sound glamorous, but embracing frugality can set you up for long-term success and financial freedom.

Living below your means simply means spending less money than you earn. It's about being mindful of your expenses, prioritizing your needs over your wants, and making conscious choices about how you use your money. While it might seem challenging at first, it's a key ingredient for building wealth and achieving your financial goals.

So, why is living below your means so important? Well, for starters, it's the foundation of financial stability. By spending less than you earn, you're able to save and invest money for the future, build an emergency fund to cover unexpected expenses, and avoid falling into debt.

Living below your means also gives you more flexibility and freedom in your life. When you're not tied down by debt or overspending, you have the freedom to make choices that align with your values and priorities. Whether it's pursuing your passions, traveling the world, or starting your own business, living below your means gives you the financial freedom to do more of what you love.

But living below your means doesn't mean living a life of deprivation or sacrifice. It's about being smart and intentional with your money, finding ways to cut costs without sacrificing the things that bring you joy and fulfillment. It might mean cooking at home instead of eating out, buying secondhand instead of brand new, or finding free or low-cost activities to enjoy with friends and family.

And remember, living below your means is a mindset, not just a temporary fix. It's about making conscious choices every day to prioritize your long-term financial well-being over short-term gratification. It might not always be easy, but with practice and perseverance, you can develop habits that set you up for long-term success and financial freedom.

So, fellow teen, are you ready to embrace frugality and start living below your means? By spending less than you earn, prioritizing your financial goals, and making smart choices with your money, you can build a solid foundation for long-term success and achieve the life of your dreams. Let's start living below our means and building our brighter financial future today!

Enjoying the Journey: Finding Happiness and Fulfillment Along the Way

While it's great to have big goals and dreams for the future, it's also important to find happiness and fulfillment in the present moment.

Life is a journey, and it's filled with ups and downs, twists and turns, and unexpected detours. And while it's natural to focus on reaching our destination, whether it's financial freedom, a successful career, or achieving our dreams, it's equally important to appreciate the journey itself.

So, how can you enjoy the journey as a teenager? Well, it starts with being present and mindful in the moment. Instead of always looking ahead to the next big thing, take some time to pause and appreciate the little things in life – like spending time with friends and family, pursuing your hobbies and interests, and experiencing new adventures.

It's also important to focus on gratitude and appreciation. Take some time each day to reflect on the things you're grateful for – whether it's a beautiful sunset, a kind gesture from a friend, or a small win in your journey towards your goals. Cultivating an attitude of gratitude can help you find joy and fulfillment in even the simplest moments of life.

And don't forget to celebrate your successes along the way. Whether it's reaching a milestone in your savings goals, achieving a personal best in your favorite hobby, or overcoming a challenge you've been facing, take some time to acknowledge and celebrate your accomplishments. It's important to recognize how far you've come and to give yourself credit for your hard work and perseverance.

But most importantly, remember that happiness and fulfillment come from within. It's not about achieving a certain goal or reaching a specific destination – it's about finding joy and meaning in the journey itself. So, don't be so focused on the future that you forget to enjoy the present moment. Take some time to slow down, appreciate the beauty of life, and savor the journey every step of the way.

So, fellow teen, are you ready to start enjoying the journey and finding happiness and fulfillment along the way? By being present, practicing gratitude, celebrating your successes, and embracing the ups and downs of life, you can create a life filled with joy, meaning, and fulfillment. Let's enjoy the journey together and make the most of every moment!